BILLY TEA & GUM LEAVE

CONTENTS

First Edition Published, October 1980
Second Edition Published, December 1982
Third Edition Published, November 1983
Fourth Edition Published, September 1985
ISBN 0 9593130 0 1

FOREWORD

I was honoured to receive Stan Dunn's invitation to write the foreword to this, his second collection of verse. Stan's very successful first publication 'Ripples on the Wannon' has given enjoyment to many who will look forward to his latest contribution.

Stan's poems reflect a deep attachment to things Australian, of today and yesterday, the land, its people and customs. They reawaken in our minds all those familiar simple memories and happenings which enrich our lives, yet are so much taken for granted.

"Poetry lifts the veil from the hidden beauty of the world and makes familiar objects be as if they were not familiar" Shelley.

This will, I believe, be just one of a succession of anthologies to flow from Stan Dunn's lively pen.

Jim Fulton
Lecturer
July, 1980.

FROM THE AUTHOR

With these verses I've used humor to help us to take a look at ourselves and our country. I feel that we are losing some of our identity.

I appreciate the encouragement so many people have given me. There could not be any better reason to share with you Billy Tea and Gum Leaves. I hope you enjoy it and that it rekindles the Aussie in us all.

With Best Wishes,

Stan Dunn

Author Stan Dunn reciting from Ripples on the Wannon

ACKNOWLEDGEMENTS

Ann Butler
Mary Davis
Tom Davis
Cynthia Dunn
Roslyn Dunn My No. 1 Fan
Jim Fulton
June Fulton
Clarice Gilchrist
Ross Gray
Meryl Limbrecht
Elsie McNicol
Jean McNicol
Jack Reid
Heather Reid
Gwen Russ
Gordon Scholz
Myrtle Scholz
Martin Willcourt
Stan Philp and Printing Staff

I appreciate greatly the time and talents that the persons listed above have given to help brew "Billy Tea and Gum Leaves."

THE MODERN ME

One time I told a certain miss
I didn't look as good as this,
In those days I could take a bow
But darling you should see me now.
My double chin is poking out,
My toes are turning up with gout,
My tongue still has too much to say
My once dark hair is turning grey.
Some say I'm daft, some say I'm clever
You, dear friend can judge whichever.
A smaller nose I would not miss,
When in my youth I tried to kiss.
Such things today I do not measure
Could I be past such youthful pleasure
My tum's too big my dear wife said
But anyhow will match my head.
Some say I'm better at my verse,
I wouldn't want to get much worse.
Perhaps it will be widely read,
When I am lying cold and dead.
If his'try brings a crown of fame,
Then I'd prefer a humble name.
So let me laugh and truly live,
Till I have no alternative.

PAM AYRES
(Sour grapes from Stan to Pam)

I'm awfully jealous of Pamela Ayres
'Cos she is so witty, yet seldom she swears,
Pam has a cute smile and a glint in her eye
That's a little bit bold and a little bit shy
She writes about people and vegies and stuff
And the reason is plain not a soul gets the huff
Pam makes us all laugh till our sides they cave in
Yet never resorts to the phrases of sin.

Pam's accent's unique and makes her a hit
I only wish I had a third of her wit,
But when she comes here and recites in our land
I'll make out I'm dumb and I don't understand.
They say she won't care if I don't like her shows
All she'll see of me is my ugly big nose,
I write about Pam and I give her plugs free
But I'll bet you a buck she won't write about me.

Pam, when you come to Aussie we'll sell you, of course
Our famous meat pies with their red bloody sauce,
We'll take you to Brisbane to back our gee gees
And watch all your fancies crawl home on their knees,
Then on Cup Day in Melbourne you can try once again
And we'll see if you laugh and write witty stuff then,
We'll take you to Sydney, you'll think it's terrific
They've got a damn bridge that spans half the Pacific.

Now there I go Pam, I am swearing dear pet,
But I've not used our great Aussie adjective yet.
You should see our 'roos spring up off their heels
All speeding so fast with their tiny front wheels,
And you'll love our Koalas so cuddly and soft
That munch only gum leaves from way up aloft.
Pam, if girls ate our gum leaves like little bears do,
Then they might get furry and cuddlesome too.

You should come in summer and see all our flies
What aren't in your plate will be stuck in your eyes,
Our jackasses laugh in our native gum trees
And our snakes are so friendly they'll fondle your knees
Now between us and snakes we've declared a détente,
'Cos Harry Butler tells us we have less than we want.
So don't take them home when you're leaving our place,
Just empty the few that have crept in your case.

Your visit to Aussie is not really funny
It's O.K. for you because you're in the money,
Your books sell like cakes on a mother's club stall
While mine sell like gum in a great opera hall,
You've sold near a million and most in your land
While me, I am hawking my first half a grand
So take your books home where they're selling red hot
Then the Aussies might buy some of my "Tommy Rot".

Pam Ayres has approved of my publishing these verses and requested a copy of
Billy Tea and Gum Leaves.

6

THE FLINDERS RANGES

Far away from concrete jungles (where the most are born and bred)
There's the charm and fascination of the Flinder's Range ahead;
The distant blue may vanish as the mysteries there unfold
Of the gorges bluffs and valleys that are rugged, steep and bold.

From Hawker up to Blinman, down below the sawtooth peaks
The relics of the squatters still remain along the creeks,
I can sense a timeless freedom in the red gums graceful spread
Like the waters underneath them as they dance along their bed.

The rockeries lace the summits in a never-ending band
To symbolize the nature of this fascinating land,
The flats are lush and verdant and are blooming wild and free
Where the showers light the valleys like the sunshine lights the sea.

When the winter cold has mellowed and the wind has lost its bite
Then the daylight hours are longer than the darkness of the night,
And the birds are busy nesting in the grass and ground and trees
As their melodies bring music to the sameness of the breeze.

The scarlet of the desert pea with single stark black eye
Seems to look from every angle like the stars do from the sky;
In the charming Flinders Ranges where the wilderness remains
That is prone to all the seasons as the ever-rolling plains.

THE COMMON FLU

My face is hot as you know what
I'm whining like a dog.
I'm pains and woe from head to toe
I'm sure I've got the wog.
My mate said drugs won't kill the bugs
But help them to endure,
So he prescribed what he described
As Granny's patent cure.

A bitter pill when you are ill
So small a price to pay,
So up I got and drank the lot
And thought it quite O.K.
To help my "Sniff" I took a whiff
Of good old Stockholm tar,
Such old time lubes will clear your tubes
Just like an enema.

I coughed a bit and had a spit
Then gargled kerosene,
Just skin and bone and all alone
And kept in quarantine.
I got the burps from drinking turps
My skin began to bubble,
My mates came in and gave me gin
To clear away the trouble.

I felt top notch on rum and scotch
And vodka straight and pure,
I took a drive, now point o five
Has undone all the cure.

I don't know what the hell I've got
My blood's about to boil,
My limbs are stiff I wonder if
My joints are out of oil.

I'm back in bed a roaring head
I've got my doctors guessing,
For near a week I could not speak
My friends said, "What a blessing".
"No sympathy for poor old me,"
I soon began to mutter,
I took my Vicks and other mix
And ate some bread and butter.

The Doc. that came gave it a name
That only pro. men knew,
Then in the end he said, "Dear friend,
You've got the common flu."
Beneath my pants he took a glance
My temp'rature to find,
He gave a dab and then a jab
Straight into my behind.

The Doc. he said, "To clear your head
A draught of aniseed
Then do a stint on peppermint
And have a decent feed."
And then he said, "You're darn near dead,
Take off your shoes and sox,
If you get worse I'll call the hearse
And place you in a box."

With such a fright I rose that night
There's nothing wrong with me,
What some folks do is nothing new
To get some sympathy.

PORT FAIRY

On the shores of Port Fairy I see the surf break
And the farmlands roll out to the Tower Hill lake
From the banks of the lake the patchwork today
Is bliss to my eyes as I scan the sea spray.
To the lowlands of Yambuk your landscape extends
And Port Fairy has charm where the Moyne River ends,
Where Wishart sailed in to its tranquil retreats
Your history spreads out from its banks to your streets,
And quaint Irish cottages stand lone in the fields
Where potatoes and onions are reaped in great yields.

Of those who came first many worshiped the cow
Others worked up the soil with their horses and plough,
They trod up the furrows turning hand over hand
Till that tender rich green was adorning their land.
They crept through their onions on hands and their knees
With the brine in their nostrils from constant south breeze,
With songs of their homeland their job it was done
In the days when their work was a part of their fun,
Their lives were so simple, their pleasures so few
But true happiness then the most Irishmen knew.

Port Fairy I wonder, how ancient are you
Are you old as your seas that reflect a deep blue?
There are men with great hopes riding high on your sea
Who bring back the catch so uncommon to me.
The fishing fleets come and the fishing fleets go
Like the passing of years and the folk that I know,
But those who came first and ploughed up this land
Are food for our memories we should understand
Their wives and their children helped till up the soil
Then family life thrived with its worship and toil.

"Others worked up the soil with their horses and plough."   Photo Courtesy: Hugh Adams, Wangoom, Victoria.

Port Fairy (Cont.)

Round Koroit and Killarney and back to the bay
Let's keep all the history that's standing today.
Refrain from excuses, we have lost it because
Preserve it right now and say this is what was
Then no matter how bleak when the wind blows a gale
We can warm a friend's heart with a good Irish tale
For an Irishman's laughter is tonic for all
In a world that's too fast and is growing too small.

BACK LEG BEN
(The Shearer's Cook and the Sydney Blonde)   1.9.85

Now Back Leg Ben was a shearer's cook
And a sort of a union fixer,
A versatile sort of bloke was Ben,
And a first class social mixer.
One day he went from the back of Bourke
To the heart of Sydney Town,
To meet a few of the social ites,
Of wide and well renown.

He finished up at a cabaret
Where they all dressed to the nines,
Where they drank less beer than a parson does
Yet pretended to know their wines.
Now Back Leg Ben had a beer or two
That gave him the urge to dance,
And he eyed this sort with a Vaucluse mob
And decided to take the chance.

Well she was as keen as a drover's dog
Cos the wines had tickled her brains,
And Back Leg Ben gave a raucus cheer
Like the frogs do when it rains.
He waltzed around the ballroom floor
With his luscious Sydney blonde,
Even though he looked as elegant
As a chook in a farmer's pond.

With one foot dragging out the back
And the other one on her toes,
His arms flapped fury to the beat
Like a pair of brawling crows.
He hugged her close to his hairy chest
The sheiler laughed and laughed,
Till Back Leg Ben yelled, "Cut it Out!
My ribs won't stand the draught."

Now Back Leg Ben was learning fast
And romance filled his eyes,
His imagination grew and grew
Till a dress was no disguise.
And then he said to his Sydney blonde
"For a girl like you I'm looking,
How about you come out West?
And help with the shearer's cooking."

Well there and then she packed her bags
And farewelled old Vaucluse,
As she posed for a snap with Back Leg Ben
For the front of the local news.
Then out to the shearers camp they went
Which was "Back of Bourke" and beyond,
To the sand and dust and flies and heat
Ben took his Vaucluse blonde.

Well, his mates all ribbed him there and then,
"Did you bring one for 'Yours Truly'
And where did you get her Ben old boy,
From Kings Cross or Kalgoorlie?"
"If you don't take her home," some grouched,
"We'll declare the whole shed black,
Cos what's the use of a shearer's cook
Laid up with a shearer's back."

Well poor Ben's problems grew and grew
Till he roared "You'll get no grub"!
And off he drove in his four-wheel drive
For a spell at the local pub.
There the barman got his eyes on the blonde
And asked her to work the till,
As the shearers flocked from near and far
And the rouse-a-bouts joined the swill.

They came from the Old "Blue Heeler" Pub,
From the Birdsville, and beyond,
They fought with knives and knuckled fists
To see who could win the blonde.
You reckon they fought over wide-comb gear
Well this was a taste of France,
Till they all discovered the Vaucluse blonde
Was a bloke in sheiler's pants.

Characters referred to in these verses are entirely ficticious.

13

THE RED CENTRE

I love all your ridges and ranges
Your ghost gums and gorges and gaps,
A paradise rare for the artist
(Some day I'll explore them perhaps),
Where the wildlife seeks refuge with water
Till the time when the wet season breaks,
Then the desert is lost in the deluge
And the creeks become series of lakes.

The red rock's akin to the ranges
As the endless red soil of the plain
Which are verdant and bloom with such splendour
Like jewels on the rugged terrain.
The wallabies home is the rockery
The red skin is king of the plain
The blue flyer's bliss to the bushman
Where the species is spared to remain.
By the wet lands the brolgas are dancing
And the eagle soars desert skies vast
As the plain turkey sprints to its freedom
On the plains that are heavily grassed.

Ayers Rock is a gigantic monster
My visions take time to conceive
It's contrast and colors and contours
Only seeing can make me believe.
Like a torchlight the sun strikes the summit
And creeps to the basement below
Till the eastern scarp fills the horizon
With its velvet soft radiant glow.

Rock Wallaby Photo Courtesy: Cynthia Dunn

Olgas Photo Courtesy: Cynthia Dunn.

The Red Centre (Cont.)

I've climbed it for mere satisfaction
And a passion to bolster my pride
And risked like the many before me
The price of a quick suicide.

But life is adventure and challenge
As we learn to receive and to give,
The folks of the outback can teach us
A lot by the way that they live.
They still have respect for the family
As they rally to help and to share
The hardships,the toil,or excitement
And compassion for those in despair.
Like the great flying Flynn of the inland
Whose courage could not be deterred
Known widely as friend and their doctor
To the blacks he was "Medicine Bird".

For a time I departed this planet
In the art Panorama by Guth
Where his masterpiece lives on the canvas
Portraying the light and the truth.
If I can't appreciate nature
And beauty eludes modern man
It's fitting we should have exceptions
And men with such talents who can.
He's depicted "The Alice" with magic
That humbles the authors and scribes
With tributes to arts and the cultures
Of the old Aboriginal Tribes.

Their ancestors home is "The Centre"
Some brand them a nuisance or cost
But who can assess the misfortune
Of a race whose identity's lost.
So the folks of the local Todd River
Are content on the river bed sand
With life styles so complex or simple
But whichever we don't understand.

When heaven's eye peeps from its cradle
As the boss of the desert and sky
It cooks like the fires of Hades
Till everything's arid and dry.
The distant horizons may vanish
The sunsets may come and depart
But forever I'll cherish the visions
That I have of the living **Red Heart**

Blue flyer*
Red Skin*   Both Species of Kangaroos

AYERS ROCK

The seasons come and the seasons go
Where the creeks all stop and the creeks all flow,
Or the dust may swirl and fill the skies
To diminish the plains of their endless size.
The Centre's a contrast cruel and kind
Separating my goal from my home behind,
When the flooding rains and the deserts wed
Each creek's a sea in a temporary bed.
They all race forth in their reckless play
In a seemingly senseless, aimless way.

Ayer's Rock is akin to the Centre's fame,
Just a simple rock with a humble name
The symbol of life on the rich red sands,
Reforming your face as the sun commands.
From a great black beast on a starlit night
To the fiery red of the firelight,
So hard to the touch yet soft to the eye
As I watch your glow in the desert sky.

I've scaled your summit where the ice winds blow
And sensed that leap to the plains below.
When the "Big Wet" laps around your base
It reflects the glow of your scarlet face.
By the verdant growth across the range,
Your Olga friends are just as strange.
As heaven's eye breaks the clouds apart,
The jewels bloom wild in the big red heart.

Everyone who comes to see our dome
Wants to take it back to their native home
The folks may come and the folks may go
But "The Rock" is ours alone to show.
Come Hell or high water and let them flock
But the world down under owns, "The Rock".

17

SCHOOLBOY CRICKET

We'd never over-rate ourselves
And yet we had some push,
And kept in mind that **Bradman** learnt
His cricket in the bush.

Although we never made the grade
We would not prod or poke,
And most our runs resulted from
Our favorite farmer's stroke.

If we were trapped out plumb L.B.
We always acted dumb,
We wore a smile of innocence
And chewed upon our gum.

Or if it hit us on the knee
We rubbed our upper arm,
And kissed our precious rabbit foot
Our treasured lucky charm.

We used a picket for a bat
Our wicket was a tin,
So those that were invincible
Would hear the horrid din.

But now my wicket's down and out
And I have had my day,
I'll watch the tests on tele' too
And tell them how to play.

FLAGSTAFF HILL — MARITIME VILLAGE

Today, those ships are monuments of sailing days so cherished
And seas that captured sailor's love where many seamen perished.
They sailed those seas and wore their faith like gentle tilted caps,
And trusted it would not be them to suffer such mishaps.

But seas reflect a friendly blue and gentle breakers roll
Till confidence is known to well in sailors with a goal.
The Loch Ard and the Schomberg, were two that met their fate
Reminding us of tragic days when hopeful friends would wait.

When sunsets were diminished, the lonely turned to pray
For those they feared had vanished and were lost to yesterday
To conquer blue horizons they relied upon their sails
Exposing all to hopeless odds in southern ocean gales.

But those who landed safely brought with them tools of trade,
'Twas from such small beginnings that this country has been made.
An anchor kindles memories of the craft both small or great
And the Peacock of the Loch Ard never fails to fascinate.

Those cliffs still stand like beacons and magnets by the shore
Disguising countless dangers of the ocean and its floor.
I sense the ocean power that overcomes all will
As history now can testify in grounds of "Flagstaff Hill".

Peacock — Photo Courtesy:
Ken Stepnell, Warrnambool.

The magnificent Loch Ard Peacock which was recovered from the sea is now on display at Flagstaff Hill Maritime Village, Warrnambool.

SHEARING AT SAM McGINTYS

I've seen the life from Darwin to the peaks of the Great Divide
From the west at old Carnarvon to the sights of Sydney-side,
I've shorn with most the shearing guns on the stations in between
But I'll vouch for Sam McGintys as the best where e're I've been.
It's not the shed, it's not the sheep, it's not the girls or beer,
It's just the yarns McGinty tells between the sheep we shear.

Sam did not learn his farming from colleges or books
He's the only farmer I have known who drenches all his chooks.
He says it stops Leucosis and bangly buckled legs
And keeps the old girls trying to lay me king size eggs;
Sam had a dog that would not work despite his pedigree
So he tied him to a buffalo's tail and set the couple free,
Said Sam, "That dog's unique today,it takes some brawn and brain
To drive a bawling buffalo from the Alice to the Plain."

Said Sam, "I sold five thousand sheep at twenty bucks a head
And then I bought five thousand more at just two bucks instead,"
Said Sam, "That's what I call a deal, a bloke like me can't lose
I've still got my five thousand sheep and lots of dough to boose"
He had a mare that would not foal so the vet did guarantee
That Sam should try some dope he had to prove its potency
The vet then asked old Sam last week, how you fairing with the dope?
Said Sam, "My doctor said last night I've still a glimpse of hope."

He thought he'd take his family to the home town of his birth
Remodelling his horse buggy to see the sights of Perth
At Cook he waited for his chance to hook it to the train
And with seat belts railway wheels and all they breezed across the Plain *
So it's not the shed it's not the sheep it's not the girls nor beer
It's just the yarns McGinty tells between the sheep we shear.

* Plain (Nullabor)   Characters referred to in these verses are entirely ficticious.

RABBITING DAYS

From boyhood days I do recall
Some memories and habits,
But none come back much clearer than
The days when I chased rabbits.
In burrows round Merino
I'll vouch without a doubt,
So I could get the ferrets in
I pulled some rabbits out.

Once came a portly lady
So friendly and so stout;
Where most old girls were laced up tight,
This old girl bulged right out.
And as she waddled through the ferns
She summoned all her strength
'Twas rare to see her feet protrude
'Neath skirt of ankle length.

She had a hat without a doubt
From Wishart's hat boutique,
The rim curled up all way around
Their "Special" for the week.
I said, "You'd like some rabbits, mum
What you would like just take."
And then she gave me cider mixed
With scrumptious Christmas Cake.

I tried to count her cats that day
Eight, ten was just a guess,
'Cos as I did five felines more
Shot out from neath her dress,
But now I knew fifteen was right,
They fought to claim a mouse,
And as they did some eighteen more
Came shooting from the house.

Old Tweedle Dum and Tweedle Dee
And Beetles, Bugs and Spider,
The old girl said, "My favorite pet
Is one called Apple Cider,"
She said, "The day I christened him
He climbed up on my hat
And next thing took a head long dive
Into the cider vat.

"I always claimed that cats can't swim
At least that's what I reckoned,
But Cider swam olympic style
Two circuits to the second."
I said "He keeps his coat so nice,"
She said, "The dear old soul,
He's always round at baking time
To lick the mixing bowl."

Rabbiting Days (Cont.)

She gasped "My God! What's wrong with you?
You look so ghostly white!"
I knew I'd caught some dizzy spell
That turned my day to night,
And as I lay half conscious-like
The old girl she did dote,
I said, "The trouble's not my tum
The lump is in my throat."

I knew I'd have to come around
Or I'd live to regret
That I once made the headlines in
Merino's social set,
I had to think of some excuse
I said, "For heavens sake
I can't be used to cider mixed
With scrumptious Christmas Cake."

"Now back to cats" the old girl said,
"I don't know girls from boys
And never keep those, "In Betweens"
To spoil their earthly joys
If they're too young to know what's what,
Or if there's any doubt,
I leave them till they're old enough
To sort the matter out."

"The secret of the color chart
Is give them lots of feed,
And you'll get brindles of all shades
When uncs and aunties breed."
So back to school on Monday morn
I hadn't many bunnies,
But still my mates were glad to hear
My bag of week-end funnies.

Characters referred to in these verses are entirely ficticious.

THE AUSSIE MONUMENT

Life out in the bush, dear friends
Is not all milk and honey,
For many a household still maintains
The good old fashioned dunny.

A gabled roof or skillion
With top and bottom vent,
And doors both at the front and back
The Aussie monument.

A distant corner of the yard
It's sited quite discreet,
And for the weekly service man
It often backs the street.

His trade is not prestigious,
His calls today are few,
Lip service like in politics
In his job would not do.

THE AUSSIE MONUMENT (Cont.)

Beneath a shady evergreen
The dunny is positioned,
So the elements of nature
Can keep it air conditioned.

And if you missed your paper boy
Who raced along the street,
You could read your pick in private
From the batch upon the seat.

The faithful Sun or Argus
Meant the owner earned a wage;
While the proper academics
Stocked the Herald or the Age.

A place to where you could escape
The office boss or phone,
With privacy to meditate
And worship all alone.

Its roof or walls may wear the scars
Of some sadistic lout,
Who stoned it till he met success
And flushed the user out.

So I guess the Aussie dunny
To most is no great joy;
But still it would have been a boon
When Adam was a boy.

THOSE OLD FAITHFUL SONGS

Today we are different
We try to depart
From the songs of gone by
That are dear to our heart;
But just to be different
Isn't nearly enough
'Cos the "Run of the Mill"
Is the any old stuff.

You can beat out a rhythm
A noise you can drum
And for a short while
There'll be many succumb;
But the old tried and true
Will live and will last
When the run of the mill
Is a thing of the past.

ADAM LINDSAY GORDON

When Gordon sought a steeple win
Some branded him a larrikin,
But now I hear a solemn bell
That stirs the air of Dingley Dell;
Few better horsemen ever were
Than he who chose to use the spur,
He cleared the fences in a stride
And rode as only boldest ride.

Gordon chanced to dent his pride
If at the big ones steeplers "Died",
The poet bold whose life was wrecked
Until we look in retrospect,
When only inches could divide
That reckless horseman in his stride,
Did horse or horseman save such fate
Let's hail the oneness of the great.

By Blue Lake waters running deep
The ghost of Gordon will not sleep,
Although at rest in Brighton grave
Immortal are the truly brave.
Though in his downs I guess he'd brood
In restless discontented mood,
Then like the leaves of spring he stirred
With lyrics like a songful bird.

With such poetic excellence
He raced his steed to clear the fence,
He spurred his mounts with great finesse
To quench his thirst for sweet success,
Did he lay claim no man should preach
The heights of fame he cannot reach.
By lake banks suicidal steep
Those words rings out from Gordon's Leap.

Home of Adam Lindsay Gordon

DINGLEY DELL

Cottage — Photo Courtesy: Mount Gambier Tourist Centre, South Australia.

HARRY BUTLER'S MATE

I've got myself a four wheel drive
And all the other needs
So I could do a "Butler" trip
Out where the wild life breeds.
With old bush hat and army boots
And rough bermuda shorts
But unlike Harry I've my doubts
If I'll attract the sorts.

At first I followed bits of dung
Of something quite profound
I sneaked around a bush or two
And there's another mound.
I traced it to a waterhole
With lots of scrub about
Just when I thought I'd trapped my prey
Two Brahman bulls charged out.

Now looking round for easy things
I scouted after frogs
So doubled back along the creek
To search beneath some logs.
I saw a big frog foot protude
So using all my guile
I grabbed and finished up in with
A three foot crocodile.

With such a fright I up the bank
To walk the bush instead
Then baking in the mid-day sun
I spied a king brown's head

I grabbed that snake behind the ears
Or where they ought to be
But then I found six feet of him
Was strangle-holding me.

But I recalled what Harry said
Don't fail to set them free
And don't destroy the living bush
That others like to see.
Unravelling him as Harry does
I soon regained my breath
Then let him go to find that I
Had choked the coot to death.

I chased a sleek goanna till
He scaled straight up a tree
Determined I'd have some success
I vouched he'd not beat me.
I up and gripped him by the tail
He dived down off a limb
And though I'm sure I 'LANDED' first
That's all I saw of him.

So then I stalked a cockatoo
And fed him beer soaked grain
Then when I saw my chance to act
I clipped him to a chain;
But he let forth a string of oaths
And some four letter word
The station wife came racing up
And said 'I stole her bird.'

With dirt and sweat from head to toe
And sunburnt legs and face
As worn out as a gum boot sock
I headed back to base.
To finish off the day I cooked
Some damper just for fun
That someone told me tasted like
A dumpling under done.

So city blokes the likes of me
Have lots of things to learn
Before they do a Butler trip
For which their hearts may yearn.
There's no two Harry Butlers mate
Though some may try like me
But next time I'll go in the wild
With Harry on T.V.

RON BARASSI

If your head has got brains
That don't relay pains,
But work like the sharpest sharp shooter,
When the boss does instruct
The message gets sucked
Straight into your giant computer.

If your chest is a box
With a heart like an ox,
And pumps like the pump on a sewer,
If your wind pipes a tunnel
That sucks like a funnel
Only oxygen healthy and pure.

There's no need to be liked,
But you must be psyched
To the point where you don't know defeat,
And you never say die
Nor even ask why
There is no team that you cannot beat.

If you're long and you're lank
And built like a tank,
And your legs will not weaken or tire,
Yet you run like a hare
And you "Smile" like a bear
While your nostrils are puffing out fire.

If your body is steel
And you lack any feel
Then you have a wonderful chassis
Now take it from me
You should go and see
Our footy coach, Ronald Barassi.

And when you're brain washed
That you can't be squashed
Just remember it's you in your skin,
When you've had your day,
What price did you pay
For the honor and glory to win?

"I am most honoured that you have firstly, composed a poem about me and then considered it for your collection for publication."
        Signed Ron Barassi

SCHOOLBOY FOOTBALL

In our schoolboy football
We played the kind of game,
That lacked the "Big Time" glamour
But we loved it just the same.
Our football was unique I guess
A novel kind of thing
Consisting of a sugar bag
Tied up with bits of string.

So when if came to bouncing it
Of course it was a dud;
At times we had to call lost ball
And search in slush and mud.
With goal posts always well defined
We did not need to mark,
They were Cootamundra wattles
And a sturdy iron bark.

To toss we'd find a piece of wood
A nicely flattened bit,
Then captain of the other side
Would call out dry or spit.
Our ground was very basic too
It did not take great skill,
Deciding when you'd won the toss
You'd kick off down the hill.

Most blokes soon learnt to hold their marks
'Cos those who didn't found,
A sugar bags elusiveness
When played along the ground.

Pee Wee and Chooka, Fred and Butch
Would always lead the play,
But "Dinga" Bell could beat us all
If he was on his day.

Unscientific was our game
But still it does intrigue,
That three of those I've named above
Went down to Melbourne league.
It goes to prove that coaching kids
And money to assist
Will not produce the footy skills
If talents don't exist.

LIFE IN THE COUNTRY TOWN

Reminding us of times gone by, a toilet stands alone
Neath an old gum tree a stable leans with a floor of cobble stone,
In the grass and dust the horse shoes rust
And the rest is overgrown.

      Once we had neighbours here and there and further down the track
      Each had a farm to call his own and a simple country shack,
      Of their where abouts I've got my doubts
      But I know they won't be back.

When buggies came with tourer cars 'twas quite a thriving town
Now shops are propped with tilted posts and old verandahs frown,
The aged are bereft and youth have left
And the place is tumbling down.

      Content with life in country towns they once remained out there
      But now the proof that they have left is lying everywhere,
      There are chimney stacks and groups of blacks
      But the white man doesn't care.

They've left to chase an endless tail, a life of modern trends
With attitudes of "Dog Eats Dog" in a world of great pretends,
So they'll never know the bonds that grow
In the lives of Outback friends.

BIRDSVILLE RACES

You may often go to races
In the cities and the towns
But you've never been to races
Till you've been to Brunette Downs,
Or the racetrack out at Birdsville
Or the turf at Barrow Creek,
Where they make a few days racing
Last a lifetime so to speak.

First they muster all the horses
From the stations far and wide
And invite the toughest horsemen
From the local country-side
You will find with outback riders
That the rivalry is great,
And their techniques tend to vary
As they thunder down the straight.

I recall one local rider
When the end was getting near
Curled his race whip like a stock whip
Round the other jockey's ear.
And there's one big rogue an outlaw
He's a stayer that can't fail
And they search the Simpson Desert
Just to bring him back to scale,

Now there's all kinds come to join us
By celebrities I've seen
Like the girls from Oodnadatta
And * The Long Bloke from Nareen.

But you'll find your social standing
Might not keep you in good stead,
If you keep reminding locals
Of the fact you're southern bred.

But you'll get hospitality
If you can play in tune
You'll be treated just like royalty
On a second honeymoon.
So why not come to Birdsville
And enjoy a beer and bet,
Where the flies get drunk as monkeys
By consuming punter's sweat;

Where the horses race like brumbies
And there's some that jib and buck,
But it adds to entertainment
For the punters out of luck
So although the Birdsville Races
May have left you all in debt
Quite unlike your city meetings
They're the ones you won't forget.

* The Long Bloke from Nareen — Malcolm Fraser

These verses relate to the Birdsville Races
of days gone by. Todays Birdsville Races are a
little more sophisticated. However reminiscing
adds a bit of flavour.
Many thanks to Pat Smith and John Finley of Quorn
for their assistance.

The Aftermath   Photo Courtesy: "Foto Fella" Don Turvey, Mildura, Victoria.

THE JOYS OF GARDENING

I'm just a harassed husband
Who loves his golf and footy,
But when the garden's left a day
My "Better Half" gets snooty.

Now I'm growing horns like snails
And biting like a bug,
I may as well live in the ground
And slither like a slug.

I start to wish I were a worm
To riggle as I please,
And then I wouldn't have to weed
Upon my hands and knees.

Those caterpillars crawl a while
And then they're flying free,
'Cos mother nature gave them wings
Not hands and feet like me.

My wife keeps busy all the week
And plants a heap of seeds,
And thinks that I'll distinguish
Her "Darlings" from the weeds.

I soak the lawn and feed it well
Its hungry roots to nourish
And then she cuts its head off
Just when it starts to flourish.

I slave away at gardening
My flowers thrive and grow
But Cyn comes out and wrecks the lot
To take them to a show.

Then she comes home a withered rose
And sniffs the smelling salts
And preaches me a sermon
On all my flower's faults.

My garden birds have ceased to sing
The bees can't find a bloom
So I'm as lonesome as a gnome
And speechless as a groom.

My "better half" has had her way
To make an exhibition
So I am off to join my mates
And do a spot of fishin'.

* Cyn (Cynthia, My wife)

CORNER OF THE STREET

A single figure seems much bigger
Than anyone else you'll meet,
If it doesn't walk or even talk
On the corner of the street.
The passers by are never shy
As some may even stare,
Would it apply if they were I
And they were standing there.

I stand and dream beside the stream
And wonder where they go,
Their shoulders brush as on they rush
I wonder who they know.
Time for chatter doesn't matter
Who cares what they say,
'Cos time that's lost is just a cost
To those I see today.

They're short and tall but one and all
Seem of a single mind,
To keep a pace with all who race
And not get far behind.
Their eager eyes may spell despise
At I who saunters on,
And as before there's always more
Replacing those who've gone.

They're up and down and round and round
As though they have a quest,
Like flies or fleas or birds or bees
Or ants that swarm the nest.
All colored skin both fat and thin
They waddle walk or run,
They weave and thread their way ahead
Till daylight's all but done.

And then the lights of city nights
A constant daylight make,
While some may sleep the rest still keep
The city wide awake.
Should we relent as we were meant
And slow the Dynamo,
Or just reguide our aimless stride
And THINK where we should go.

THE FARMERS LAMENT

This year my pigs can't win a prize
My chooks are laying undersize,
The wife has got a bout of flu
I'll bet the kids all get it too,
I've got the gout in all my toes
They say that's how the farm life goes,
I've seen a drought and also flood
And worked to eye balls in the mud,
I slave my heart out day and night
But nothing seems to turn out right.

The rooster's lousy now with lice
The cats are sick of catching mice,
Last year so thickly they did swarm
They slept with cats so they'd be warm,
Last week I got my dog de-flead
And now my hack has gone knock kneed,
My tractor batteries gone ka-put
I've bills galore that I can't foot,
My hair on top is growing thin
I think I'll cash the whole lot in.

The bank has broken on the dam
On Monday last I lost my ram,
I went and told the maiden ewes
And all they said was "Marvellous News,"
My bull has caused me more expense
By busting through the neighbour's fence,
His cows displayed their courting game
But boys they always get the blame,
My neighbour raved for near a week
And now the neither of us speak.

The women round about us talk
About the newly-weds and stork,
They have their fun at mother's club
While we are joking at the pub,
All share around what are their views
And catch up on the local news,
It does us all a lot of harm
To criticize the neighbour's farm,
We manage worst our own affairs
But we're experts at running theirs.

To boost the cows we need some rain
But hope it's dry to harvest grain,
We pray for wind to work the mill
But for our crops we want it still,
Dear weather man you are excused
'Cos we ourselves are so confused,
In our cow yard the cow pollutes
The little bits around our boots,
But we can't take your city smog
That isn't fit for man or dog!

I hope by when this showtime ends
The "Bush" and "Big Smoke" both are friends,
I've tried to help you understand
A cocky's life upon the land,
I've really meant to educate
And help us to assimilate,
The price of grain and meat and wool
Is always UN-PRE-DICT-A-BULL,
We moan and groan and whine and wail
But still the farm is not for sale.

ARTIFICIAL BREEDING

On artificial breeding the experts have their say
They treat us all like ornaments, us bulls of modern day.
We know that its inventor was a mean and nasty bloke,
And all us bulls are fired up and breathing jet black smoke.
Our cow friends now will all go dry, without romantic charm
Then who will there be left to pay the debts upon the farm?
So cows today should hold their milk and keep their masters rationed
Till they consult and all agree that cows can be old fashioned.
How would men like wedding days that go all afternoon
And then the bride goes home to Mum without the honeymoon?

THE FENCER- LEN ANDERS

His cap was tilted on his head
He chewed upon his gum,
He swore and cursed and said the worst
Till ev'ry post was plumb.
His bulky frame with giant hands
That gripped like foundry vice,
He crushed me when we met first time
But never caught me twice.

His posts are rammed so straight in line
A column from behind,
And from the side are soldier boys
Well spaced and upright lined.
The wire's threaded through the holes
At gauge that he commends,
It's joined up with a figure eight
With no untidy ends.

His gates are swung like sentry doors
Not cocky gates I've found
That take some science to undo
And brawn to swing them round,)
They swing today, they've swung for years,
They'll swing for years to come,
Cos the strainers have them anchored
To perfection true and plumb.

He worked for men up Woolsthorpe way
Who wisely spent their pence
And got the man they knew was best
To build the stockyard fence.
Jack Douglas, Askew, White and Co.,
The Ross's and Bob Hood,
They got the man to build their fence
As only Leonard could.

The fence post shadows now grow long
They fade and disappear,
But when the sun comes up next day
The shadows re-appear.
And that's the way Len Anders is
He's put away his gear,
But ride out where the fence line is
And you'll find Len is here.

But if you don't believe me
Just ask the boundary men,
And they will vouch my claim is true
They often see dear Len.
Some may forget our Len a while
But in the decades hence,
His name will live synonymous
With those who ride the fence.

Len Anders was undoubtedly one of Australia's
Best farm fencing contractors.
He always said, "Near enough is not good enough.
The only way to do it is the right way."

These verses are published with the kind permission of his family.

JOHN AND JULIE

Out along the Birdsville Track
Where the Queensland heelers bark
John and Julie are romancing
In the salt bush after dark.
And then they went to Sydney
To honeymoon a week,
But Johnny he went walk-a-bout
When people would not speak.

Dear Julie searched for Johnny
But she was at a loss,
So for a moment waited
On a corner in King's Cross.
The lads all flocked around her
And plastered her with dough,
They kissed her cheeks and held her arms
And would not let her go.

When she knew their intentions
That they were not her kind,
She took off like an emu
With a dingo pack behind.
She reached the Sydney Harbour
Which seemed to change her luck,
As she flagged down the driver
Of a Winton Queensland truck.

He kept his motor roaring
All through the lonely night,
And made his home town Winton
As day was breaking light.

He said "I'd better check this rig
Before the Birdsville track,"
And when he did, found fifty blokes
Were riding on the back.

He raced on to the Birdsville pub
John gave them all a show,
While Julie sneaked out to the yard
And let the heelers go
Those fellas with their stubbies
Took off across the plain,
And did not stop till Boulia
Where they caught a cattle train.

Some clambered in the cabin
A sea of legs and arms
And the rest got in the trailers
With the Santas and the Brahams.
When they got back to Sydney
They'd a story of their own,
How dear Julie of the outback
Had worn them skin and bone.

The moral of my story is
We all are birds and bees,
But let's show a little kindness
To our Aborigines.
Then way out on the Birdsville track
Where the Queensland heelers bark
John and Julie can romance in peace
In the salt bush after dark.

Characters referred to in these verses are entirely ficticious

Humorous as they may seem, these verses reflect a few thoughts which came to me while in Central Australia in 1979. The problems of the Aboriginal people are far too complex for my simplistic views. Unlike innocent Julie however, WE take for granted the complexities of our modern society. There are many areas where kindness and understanding can restore trust which is vital to nation, race and individual if the wheels of humanity are to turn smoothly. The monetry cost would be nought. The returns could be priceless.

TO THE MEMORY OF MY PARENTS

All the chips are wet and sodden
But the bark begins to flare
To revive nostalgic mem'ries
Of the billy tea we'd share,
When the magpies scouted round us
With their cadging kind of calls
Where my mother spent her childhood
By the Wannon River falls.

In a little red roof cottage
Which was quite a common style
With her sisters and her brother
She would walk a country mile,
They knew the simple pleasures
And the pranks of childhood play
Then they seemed far more contented
Than the children of today.

With their horses and their buggies
All the neighbours shared their joys
In the dance halls of the district
On the night when girls met boys.
Then the girls would line the side walls
Till the dancers rocked the floors
And the surplus lads stood laughing
Telling yarns around the doors.

Now my father was no dancer
But with horses showed his skills
As he cleared the logs and fences
Round Tahara's steepest hills.
In the moment of his glory
With the satin and the lace
Old Bill brought home his colors
In the Western Steeplechase.

There were many horses faster
But when jumping skills applied
Matchless Bill emerged the master
As he cleared them in his stride.
There are some who still remember
And rekindle many tales
Of the bullock and the rider
When they jumped the post and rails.

It was there they raced their horses
Through the farmlands far away
Where the red gums slept majestic
And they're sleeping still today.
So the birth place of my forbears
Is imprinted in my mind
And my pride will always flourish
With the names they've left behind.

These lines are dedicated to the memory of my Father and Mother, Ray and
Florence Dunn.

Author's parents Ray and Florence Dunn in their youth.

THE WORKING MAN

I am just a common worker
In my overalls of grime,
I often used to wonder
If I came before my time.
When I think of Dad before me
And how he used to slave,
I guess I should be thankful
Not stir, and rant and rave.

But my age is catching up with me
I'm aches from head to toe;
But still I keep on slaving
At the only work I know.
I've dug in holes and tunnels
I've never been a shirker,
And I'll never be a rich man
But I'll always be a worker.

The Governments and Unions
Stab each other in the back,
Some say we workers work too long
But many say we're slack.
For those who sit in Parliament
And don't get even soiled,
Come and join me in the tunnel
And you'll know that you have toiled.

"My job is complimentary
To the lawyer, boss and king"
Well, it's nice of you to say so
But it doesn't mean a thing!
For there's many blokes work shorter
And their pays in steps and stairs,
So if I'm worth as much as them
I'll swap them mine for their$.

45

MT ISA (THE ISA BURNS TONIGHT)

The Aussies of "The Isa" are a special kind of breed
And extend the hand of friendship to all colors, class and creed,
As that wealth is daily surfaced from the tunnels deep below
Where they share the kind of comradeship as only miners know,
And they tell the world their story of the one John Frederick Miles
Whose memory is projected 'bove the normal rank and files
'Neath the cloudless skies of Isa where his pack horse chanced to stray
Now his soul relives the glory of that priceless yesterday.

Out amongst the rocky outcrops your horizons wear the scars
And your chimney stacks are neighbours with the moonlit skies and stars.
The Leichhardt river's sleeping but so wildly it can flow
Just as though the brutes in Hades let a bag of serpents go,
But your family life is foremost as you share that common goal
To keep the rockface tumbling in that endless winding hole,
And your lookout stirs my childhood with the streets all blazing bright,
Making patterns interwoven as "The Isa" burns tonight.

Photo Courtesy: Mount Isa Mines, Queensland.

US AND OUR COUNTRY

Many a man has swung his swag and taken to the bush
And put up with adversity away from city push,
They've trudged across the country side to stations way out back
When all their worlds possessions were the contents of a sack.

They chased the shearing shed to shed or swept the greasy board
And oft' were paid and fed much less than squatters could afford,
Is it for better or for worse that swagmen now have died?
For every one who grafted there were many more who tried.

So few then found their fortune but let there be no doubt
They learned from sheer adventure what the world was all about,
Today we crowd our cities and the self sufficient fade
It's just too bad for drop outs who have never made the grade.

Do we seek to climb the ladder with a closed and rigid mind?
And never cross the boundaries that our training has defined.
Should we take a leaf from forbears who failed to pass the test?
Yet found in life their calling in the talents they possessed.

I sympathise with jobless who are living on the dole
The road of self destruction of the body, mind and soul,
Will our cities be our downfall where the poor and helpless hide
Will life have lesser meaning now the world is not so wide.

Let's hope there'll be compassion and the winds of fortune blow
Till the men of greater vision urge us all to have a go,
Or will we cling like termites to the hallowed coastal strips
Till the swagmen march in columns with their holsters on their hips.

AUSSIE PUB CRAWL

An Aussie's a bloke
Who can share a good joke
Or a beer with the boys now and then,
When his gee gees have lost
He'll not winge at the cost
In the pub bars from six until ten.

When a wife he has caught
He still loves his old sport
That takes him away with the men,
And if she should moan
Then his time is his own
In the pub bars from six until ten.

Oh how are ya' mate
Is a welcome that's great
I hear it again and again,
From the man on the street
To the cop on the beat
Or in pub bars from six until ten.

The barman he sweats
For the quid that he gets
While the maid clucks around like a hen,
Her shapely young hips
Win the customers tips
In the pub bars from six until ten.

The towny may boast
Of a shack on the coast
Where he spends a few days now and then,
And the wool cheques they rise
Like the dust and the flies
In the pub bars from six until ten.

From the swag on his knees
To the bloke with degrees
Or the fellow who pushes the pen,
From the bum to the snob
You will meet the whole mob
In the pub bars from six until ten.

STUNTS AT KATHERINE

Have you ever been to Katherine
To see the raft race fours,
Where regulations stipulate
A tiolet brush for oars
And also up at Katherine
They tell me, "Now by George",
A fella rode his motorbike
Across the Katherine Gorge

*crocs (crocodiles)

And when he got half way across
He parked his bike on rocks
And caught himself a fish or two
To feed the hungry crocs*
He then rode up the other bank
And showed a lovely barra*
A stunt I'd thought impossible
Except on Melbourne's Yarra.

*barra (barramundi fish)

Raft race fours Katherine

John Pfitzer's motor bike stunt

Special thanks to Glenda Toogood, Lorraine O'Neil, Heather and Steve Jenner for supplying photos and assisting me with my research.

John did actually ride his motor bike across the Katherine River at Katherine by wearing snorkel etc. and welding a big exhaust to his motor bike which was modified for the stunt.

OUR MELBOURNE OF TODAY

At the Melbourne cup
We can play it up
And laugh although we lose,
We can blame the course
Or the rocking horse
Joe Brown picked on the news.

When the Navy Blues
And the Kangaroos
Play before one hundred grand,
Who all have their say
How their teams should play
From their perches in the stand.

CHORUS
So now one and all
Come and have a ball
Where the lights are bright and gay,
We can join the throng
And feel we belong
To our Melbourne of today.

And when Moomba comes
Dads and kids and mums
Come to join the fun in store,
And the dragon meets
All who line the streets
Where there's gaiety galore.

We can dance and sing
Like the birds in spring
There is so much to be found,
If we'll take and give
We can start to live
On the Melbourne Merry-Go-round.

CHORUS

And to herald spring
Country cousins bring
A breath of spring time air,
When the stock and land
Always look so grand
At our giant spring time fair.

And we love to show
All the things we grow
And the crafts that we have made,
And the stock we breed
That we ride or lead
In the Melbourne show parade.

CHORUS

Music: Courtesy Cynthia Dunn

YABBIE YARNS

When the N. T. folks direct you a short way down the track
Allow yourself a week or two to get down there and back
Now if you're keen on fishing just try the river Todd
And you'll know you have patience by the time you've caught a cod.

    The lads from round the Alice when they've had too many beers
    Race up and down the river Todd with boats around their ears.
    The girls from outback stations are a special kind of breed,
    They ride the Santas shopping till they're tame enought to lead.

The cattle trains out this way are so long from front to back
When their motors at the Three Ways their tail's on Birdsville track.
If you love an egg flip just try our outback dregs
Like our Diamentina cocktail, *roo milk and emu's eggs.

    The *'crocs don't like the locals when it comes to choice of platter,
    They prefer to dine on tourists who are better fed and fatter.
    When *'roos swarm round at sunset, the Yankies look quite vague,
    But locals soon convince them, we've a mammoth locust plague.

*N. T. (Northern Territory)
*'roos (Kangaroos)
*'crocs (Crocodiles)

RIPPLES ON THE WANNON
Australiana Verse

Ripples on the Wannon has exceeded all expectations selling over **14,000** copies. Widely travelled it has gone all over Australia and to several overseas countries. By the response, Ripples on the Wannon has carried with it much good will. I have enjoyed meeting so many people in pen and person.

I am very grateful to Cynthia, my wife, who has tolerated me reciting in my sleep and also to Roslyn, my daughter, and most enthusiastic fan.

Sincere thanks to all who assisted and I am confident Ripples on the Wannon will be around for some time to come.

If unavailable at your newsagent, contact the author.

CONTENTS INCLUDE

The Long Bloke From Nareen
The Grampians
Steeplechasing in Western Victoria
Old Man Murray
Kalgoorlie
The Outtram Sons (Stan & Jack)
Tasmania
Warrnambool ("Playground of the South")
Song Of Australia
Wahgunyah By The Murray
Merino Forever

Sydney Beats Them All
Mildura
The Warrnambool Grand Annual Steeplechase
Pioneering Days
The Hills Of Coleraine
Sunny Perth
Marysville
How Not To Milk A Cow
and many more